1112

CR

Healthy HABITS™

Maintaining a Healthy Weight

Kate Canino

New York

To Rachel Chaffee, who has been my stable friend for over twenty years. When it comes to healthy eating, finding new recipes, and cooking, you have and always will be an inspiration.

Published in 2011 by The Rosen Publishing Group, Inc.
29 East 21st Street, New York, NY 10010

First Edition

Library of Congress Cataloging-in-Publication Data

Canino, Kate.
Maintaining a healthy weight / Kate Canino.—1st ed.
    p. cm.—(Healthy habits)
Includes bibliographical references and index.
ISBN 978-1-4358-9439-6 (library binding)
ISBN 978-1-4488-0609-6 (pbk)
ISBN 978-1-4488-0618-8 (6-pack)
1. Health—Juvenile literature. 2. Body weight—Juvenile literature. 3. Diet—Juvenile literature.
4. Physical fitness—Juvenile literature. I. Title.
RA777.C28 2011
613—dc22

2009053186

Manufactured in Malaysia

CPSIA Compliance Information: Batch #S10YA: For further information, contact Rosen Publishing, New York, New York, at 1-800-237-9932.

CONTENTS

Introduction

Establishing healthy habits at a young age means living a long and healthy life. Such habits include wholesome eating, exercising, taking time out for oneself, and seeking out family and friends who encourage and support these healthy practices. When people lead healthy lives by developing these habits, they may discover that they have more energy, motivation, and self-esteem, as well as the confidence to try new things.

The key to keeping these healthy habits is to become part of a community of people who also want to be healthy. Find family members, friends, and others in your social circle who would be good role models. When a commitment is made to leading a healthy lifestyle (whether alone or with a group), many benefits can be achieved for both the mind and the body. Having a support network will be an encouragement on those tough days.

Being active in the community is important to a person's well-being, too, since it allows a person to move outside of his or her own world and help others. Young adults can get wrapped up in trying to be popular, wearing the right clothes, and having the newest technology. When one is volunteering in the community or doing something as simple as helping a neighbor take the garbage out, it's a way to avoid selfishness and worrying about superficial things. When people feel better about themselves and how they contribute to this world, they are more likely to take better care of their bodies. There are many ways that an individual can volunteer his or her time. Check with the community centers, schools, churches, and other nonprofit organizations in

Volunteering is a terrific way to make new friends and have a positive impact within the community, which can allow a person to feel better about himself or herself.

your area to find ways that you can give your time. Also, the Web site Volunteer Match (http://www.volunteermatch.org) will match people up with volunteer positions based on their ZIP code and area of interest.

Starting to build healthy habits now will help prevent a sedentary lifestyle and diseases in the future. The main concern for young adults might be the here and now, but making the necessary changes now to prepare their bodies for the future will help ensure a long, full, and healthy life. A sedentary lifestyle is one in which a person engages in very little, if any, physical activity and does a lot of sitting around. Leading a sedentary lifestyle and practicing other unhealthy habits increases the possibility of acquiring adult onset diseases such as heart disease, obesity, type 2 diabetes, and sleep apnea. This book will give young adults the tools they need to control their weight and lead a healthy lifestyle now and in the future.

Chapter 1

The Importance of Controlling Weight

As a young adult, controlling one's weight affects the rest of the body because it's going through so many changes. Young adults will naturally put on weight due to hormone changes. When your body reaches the stage we call puberty, the brain releases a hormone called gonadotropin-releasing hormone, or GnRH for short. This hormone, in turn, releases two more puberty hormones called luteinizing hormone (LH) and follicle-stimulating hormone (FSH). All of these new chemicals move around inside the body, giving it adult-level hormones.

Due to the influx of new hormones, some young adults will gain weight more quickly during this time as the amounts of muscle, fat, and bone in their bodies change. All of the new weight a young adult gains during adolescence is completely natural and healthy as long as his or her body fat, muscle, and bone are the right proportion. That is why regular checkups with a health care professional are so important: A person knows he or she is on the right track to a healthy weight.

Extra body fat helps in the growth process during this time because the body needs the energy of stored fat to grow. In order to control the weight that a young adult puts on during this stage of his or her life, eating and exercising properly is very important. The key to maintaining weight is not allowing caloric intake to exceed the

As a young adult, it is perfectly natural to put on weight to help the body in its growth process. Health care professionals are there to help you maintain a healthy weight and to educate you on the proper amount of weight you should or should not gain.

number of calories burned during exercise. When calories consumed are more than those burned, the body starts to put on weight. Also, not putting too much pressure on oneself to look a certain way and surrounding yourself with positive role models will make help you sustain a healthy weight.

Be careful of trying to obtain the "ideal" body that magazines and television portray. Hollywood's idea of physical beauty is rarely, if ever, attainable. The pictures of celebrities in magazines are fixed up to look "perfect." Also, celebrities have makeup artists and stylists to help them look that way, and they spend anywhere from two to three hours getting ready for a photo shoot or a movie scene. People should not measure themselves against others. If someone is concerned about putting on weight too quickly, he or she should seek advice from a health care professional.

How to Control Weight

As a young adult, you might be concerned about what the "right weight" is. Everybody's body is unique. We are all shaped in a variety of ways, metabolize food differently, and enjoy different forms of exercise. If everyone in the world looked the same, ate the same, and enjoyed the same activities, life would be fairly dull. Controlling weight is a popular topic because of all the pressure that society places on young adults to look and act a certain way. An essential way to control weight is finding out what motivates a person to get off the couch and take the steps necessary to learn how to build healthy habits.

There are always ups and downs in life, and it may not always be easy. However, when a person is motivated to do something, he or she is more likely to succeed. Take the time and write down all of the

Taking the time to think about and write down the things that are important to you is a significant way to stay positive and motivated.

things that make life an enjoyable experience. Write down your favorite types of exercises, favorite foods, and the friends and family members you enjoy doing these things with. Gaining a sense of identity is important to one's self-esteem.

This is a time when teens are trying to figure out who they are, how they fit into the world, and what they want in life. The important thing to do is remain positive and find good role models to be inspired by. A true role model is someone who has the qualities that one would like to obtain. A role model motivates someone to be a better person

Asking Questions

Here are some questions to spark interest in the benefits of controlling one's weight:

- What types of exercises or physical activities do I enjoy?
- Who can I ask to join me in these activities?
- What is the motivation for me to control my weight?
- What things in life inspire me?
- What kinds of healthy foods do I like?
- Who can I talk to if I am unsure of what I need to do to maintain a healthy weight and build good habits?

Answering these questions will give anyone a head start on what needs to be done to control his or her weight, and they will direct a person to where he or she needs to go to build healthy habits. Share these questions and answers with a role model so that he or she can help you stay accountable or give suggestions on how to get started.

and make the right choices in life. Here are some questions to spark interest in the benefits of controlling one's weight:

Do I Need to Lose Weight?

Young adults should be at a weight where they feel healthy and happy, not at a weight where they have to starve or exercise fanatically in order to maintain it. According to *Trim Kids*, by child weight expert Melinda Sothern, it is normal for young adults to gain an average of 3 to 5 pounds (1.4 to 2.3 kilograms) for every inch that they grow. A girl's growth spurt starts between the ages of ten and twelve and can

Before contemplating a diet of rice cakes and water, seek out the help of a physician or nutritionist so that he or she can tailor a diet that will give you all the nutrients you need for a healthy body.

end anywhere between the ages of seventeen and nineteen. A boy's growth spurt begins anywhere from ages twelve to fourteen and ends at about age twenty. If teens are gaining more weight than normal or none at all, it may be the right time to seek out a health care professional so that they can be sure they are on the right track.

Everyone is different. According to Anne M. Fletcher, author of *Weight Loss Confidential*, "Children come into the world with a genetic tendency toward a certain shape and weight, but their families' habits also help determine how they grow and develop." It is up to each individual to control food choices and the amount of physical activity that he or she is getting. If the cupboards in the house are filled with food that is not as nutritional as it could be, encourage family members to start eating more healthfully. Together, research fun recipes or snacks that can be kept in the house. It is always more fun when family members are involved because more ideas can be generated. If there is no one around that is able to help, find a neighbor or friend that can help you make good choices. According to Fletcher, some factors that can cause a person to gain weight are:

- Too much snacking
- Portion sizes are too large
- Not enough exercise
- Too many sweets and desserts
- Emotional causes (lonely, bored, sad)
- Too much time in front of the TV or computer; video games
- Too much fast food

Each of these factors can cause a person to put on more weight, especially if he or she is not exercising. If one or more of these categories describes you or someone you know, maybe it is time to make some changes in your life. The benefits of controlling weight are that a person will feel better about himself or herself as a young adult. Physically, the body will feel better and function better because it is not in a constant state of flux. There are serious consequences when someone is not able to control his or her weight. It can cause many health problems in the present, as well as into adulthood. It could affect a person for the rest of his or her life.

Possible Effects of Being Overweight

In the last thirty years, a growing number of young people have developed weight problems. Today, one out of three kids and teens between the ages of twelve and nineteen are overweight or obese, meaning that a person is very overweight. Overweight or obese means that a person is carrying around more body fat than what is healthy for his or her age and height. A doctor is the best person to determine whether or not one needs to lose or gain weight. Even if a person feels like he or she is at a good weight, it is still good to receive regular checkups to ensure that one is getting proper nutrition. Some of the conditions that a young adult can develop due to being overweight and/or obese, according to the Centers for Disease Control and Prevention (CDC), are:

- **Coronary artery disease.** This disease involves the narrowing of the small blood vessels that supply blood and oxygen to the heart. This occurs when fatty material builds up on the walls of your arteries (plaques), causing the vessels to narrow, thus limiting the blood flow to the heart.

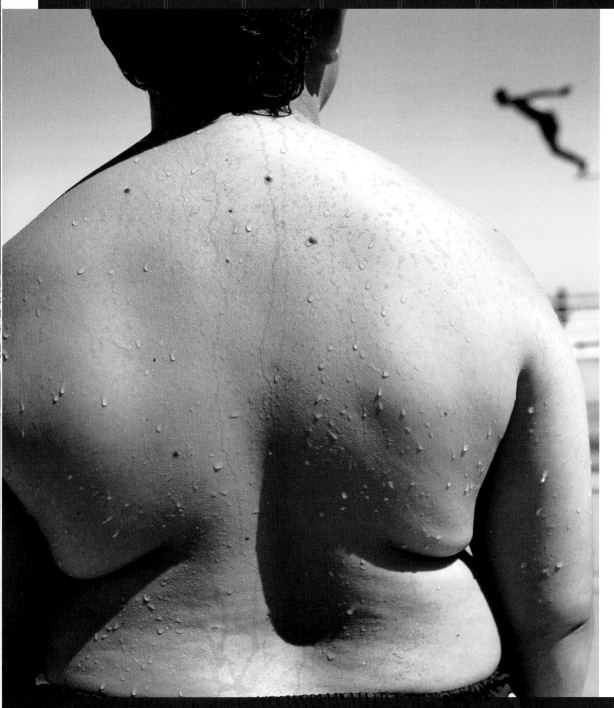

Many young adults struggle with being overweight, which can lead to adult onset diseases, but there are a number of ways to get healthy and maintain a healthy weight.

- **Type 2 diabetes.** Formerly called non-insulin-dependent diabetes, type 2 diabetes is increasingly being found in children and adolescents and is directly linked to increasing childhood obesity. Diabetes is one of the main causes of death in the United States, and it causes devastating complications, such as kidney disease and blindness.
- **High blood pressure.** High blood pressure is when the heart and arteries have a much heavier workload, causing the heart to pump harder. The heart and its arteries may no longer work as well as they should if this continues for a long period of time.
- **Obstructive sleep apnea.** This breathing disorder is defined as the breath stopping during sleep for at least ten seconds. It is often characterized by loud snoring and labored breathing. When a person suffers from sleep apnea, the oxygen levels in his or her blood can fall dramatically as he or she temporarily stops breathing.

There are also risks to one's self-esteem and self-worth that are related to being overweight. According to the CDC, obese children and adolescents are targets of early social discrimination. The stress of being teased about one's weight can cause low self-esteem, which, in turn, can hinder the way in which a young adult interacts socially as well as performs academically.

Young adults often encounter people taunting them about their looks because one's appearance seems to be everything during the teenage years. It is important to surround oneself with peers who are encouraging and talk positively about others. A person never knows what another person's problems may really be. Therefore, one should

Speaking positively about oneself is extremely important for the self-image of a young adult. Those who may struggle with their appearance need support and encouragement from friends.

be careful about what is said. If there is concern for yourself or for a friend, seek the help of a teacher, adult, or family member.

The reason why young adults should start learning to control their weight now is that it will be easier for them to maintain a healthy life-style later in life. Making the proper food choices and learning how to prepare food that a person enjoys will come in handy as a person gets older. It is important that one is aware of both the negative and positive components in various foods so that educated decisions can be made about what is put into the body. Healthy habits will already be established and can be built upon as more information and the introduction to new foods and cuisines are experienced. When a teenager makes wise food choices and exercises regularly, the results can last a lifetime.

Chapter 2

Eating Right

Wholesome eating is essential to keeping our bodies functioning properly. Healthy food is the fuel that keeps our internal engines going. Eating healthy means consuming lots of fruits, vegetables, and grains. It doesn't mean a person can't have a sweet treat every once in a while, but people should eat such foods in moderation. Think twice before eating, and find out what the ingredients are, check labels, and don't be afraid to ask someone if what you are eating has any nutritional value. Sometimes a person needs something sweet to eat. Therefore, when a choice needs to be made and that candy bar seems to be calling your name, eat half of it and save the rest for tomorrow. Or try drinking a glass of water and waiting ten minutes to see if the desire to eat is still there. Sometimes the body craves sweet treats because blood sugar levels are low, so it is a matter of finding healthy ways to raise those sugar levels.

Everything put into the body has either a positive or negative effect. Therefore, you are what you eat. When foods that are healthy and have a high nutritional value are chosen, a person will have a sustainable amount of energy to move and grow. When people eat a lot of junk food that is high in sugar and calories, their energy levels will spike and crash, leaving them feeling lethargic and without the nutrients their bodies need to grow properly.

Choosing a variety of healthy foods will keep the taste buds satisfied and give a person the inspiration to try new foods and keep a balanced diet.

The food a person consumes affects the body in many different ways. A healthy diet gives a person energy that is sustainable through-out the day, while an unhealthy diet tends to make a person ultimately feel tired and sluggish.

The word "diet" can sometimes have a negative meaning. We are a society that is obsessed with having perfect bodies. In this book, though, "diet" means the types of foods that a person eats regularly. There are ways to control weight by changing diet based on what kind and how much food a person consumes. Some people need more calories than others. A health care professional can help a person decide how many calories to consume and how to best consume them. Just because it's recommended that a person consume 1,500 calories per day doesn't mean those calories should come from soda, pizza, and ice cream. A healthy diet is a balanced one where calories are taken in from all sorts of foods.

Eating right is extremely important in order to prevent too much weight gain. Food is the energy for the body, just like gas is fuel for a car. It is the fuel that keeps the body moving, and it gives the body the nutrition it needs to repair itself. That is why proper nutrition is key to maintaining a healthy weight. Putting the wrong kind of gas in your car can ruin the engine, just like putting the wrong food in your body can cause it to break down and not work properly. Young adults need proper nutrition to have the energy to do everything from playing sports to having the mental energy to do schoolwork.

The Three Main Components of Food

There are three main components in food that the body absorbs in order to function properly. Those three components are carbohydrates, proteins, and fats. The carbohydrates that you get from foods such as bread and pasta provide energy for you to be active. There are two types of carbohydrates, simple and complex carbohydrates. Simple carbohydrates, also known as simple sugars, are found mainly in

Carbohydrates seem to have a bad reputation for those trying to control their weight, but it is the type and amount of carbohydrates that one puts in the body that can have a positive or negative result.

refined sugars. Refined sugar is the white sugar that one can find in a sugar bowl. If a person eats gummy bears, a lollipop, or drinks a soda, he or she is consuming simple carbohydrates. Simple sugars can also be found in more nutritious foods, such as fruit and milk,

which are healthier sources because these foods also contain vitamins, fiber, and important nutrients like calcium.

The second type of carbohydrate is complex carbohydrates, also called starches. Starches include grain products, such as bread, crackers, pasta, and rice. There are healthy choices of complex carbohydrates. Refined grains include flour and white rice. They are grains that have been processed. Refining removes nutrients and fiber. Unrefined grains, though, keep their vitamins and minerals and are rich in fiber, which helps the digestive system. When fiber is absorbed into the body, it helps a person feel full. As a result, one is less likely to overeat. Both of these types of carbohydrates should be part of a healthy diet. It is just a matter of choosing the right ones. The key is to limit the amount of simple sugars and eat more complex carbohydrates. Some complex carbohydrates are vegetables, whole-grain bread, and oatmeal.

Another main component the body gains from food is protein. This is essential to one's diet because it helps the body build up, maintain, and replace tissues. Your muscles, organs, and immune system are all made up mostly of protein. The best sources of protein are legumes like black beans, dairy products, nuts, eggs, fish, poultry, and beef. According to KidsHealth.org, the body uses the proteins that you eat to "make lots of specialized protein molecules that have specific jobs." For

Fish is an amazing source of protein to add to one's diet. Shopping at a local fish market can be a little stinky, but it's fun to see all the different types of fish there are to choose from.

instance, the body makes hemoglobin from protein. This is the part of the red blood cells that takes oxygen to every single part of the human body. Some other proteins are used to build muscle in your heart. They also help in the movement of the legs and lungs.

Fat is the means by which the body is fueled and able to absorb vitamins. It also contains the building blocks of hormones and helps insulate nervous system tissue. Fat seems to get a bad reputation in American society, but some fat is necessary to maintain a healthy diet. The secret is to get the fat that the body needs from lean meats, fish, and oils that are healthy to the heart. There are three types of fat:

1. Unsaturated fats. These are found in plant foods and fish and are "healthy fats." The best sources of unsaturated fats are olive oil, peanut oil, canola oil, albacore tuna, and salmon.
2. Saturated fats. These fats can be found in meat and other animal products, such as butter, cheese, and all milk, except skim milk. Saturated fats are also in palm and coconut oils, which are often used in baked goods that you find in the store. Eating too much saturated fat can raise blood cholesterol levels and increase the risk of heart disease.

Knowing how different foods help control weight is important as young adults take on more responsibility for their well-being.

3. Trans fats. These fats can be found in margarine, especially the kind that comes in sticks. Trans fats are also found in certain foods that you buy at the store or in a restaurant, such as snack foods, baked goods, and fried foods. When you see "hydrogenated" or "partially hydrogenated" oils on an ingredient list, the food contains trans fats. Trans fats are listed on the food label. Like saturated fats, trans fats can raise cholesterol and increase the risk of heart disease.

Sometimes it would probably seem easier to just pop a pill to provide all of these nutrients, as opposed to having to think about all of these things and then coming up with a way to make the food and eat it. However, if a person looks at it as a fun way to stay healthy, all of a sudden food can be a way to enjoy one of life's greatest traditions. Eating can be a great social event that includes people you enjoy in life. Food can be comforting as well as satisfying.

Why Our Bodies Need "Smart" Food Choices

It is essential that the diet of a young adult contains proper nutrition. Food not only gives a person energy, but it also supplies the building blocks to rebuild and repair the cells in the body. The body is in a constant state of being broken down. Therefore, a person needs to eat in order to rebuild it. Consuming foods that have the ability to supply the proper building blocks will guarantee that the body grows at a healthy rate. Shopping smart will aid in proper nutrition as well as controlling one's weight.

A healthy eating plan includes an emphasis on fruits, vegetables, whole grains, and fat-free or low-fat milk and milk products. It includes

		fortified skim milk	Ch U
Calories			
Calories from Fat	120	160	
	15	15	
Total Fat 1.5g *	% Daily Value**		
Saturated Fat 0g	2%	2%	1
Trans Fat 0g	0%	2%	0g
Polyunsaturated Fat 0.5g			0g
Monounsaturated Fat 0.5g			0g
Cholesterol 0mg			0g
Sodium 160mg	0%	1%	0mg
Potassium 90mg	7%	9%	110mg
Total Carbohydrate 25g	3%	8%	60mg
Dietary Fiber 2g	8%	10%	16g
Soluble Fiber 1g		8%	1g
Sugars 6g			1g
Other Carbohydra			<1g
Protein 3g			4g
			11g
			1g

Protein		
Vitamin A	0%	
Vitamin C	0%	
Calcium	10%	
Iron	45%	
Thiamin	25%	3
Riboflavin	25%	40%
Niacin	25%	25%
Vitamin B6	25%	30%
Folic Acid	60%	70
Phosphorus	10%	60% 110%
Zinc	25%	25% 15%
		30% 80%

*Amount in Cereal. One half cup skim milk contributes an
additional 65mg Sodium, 200mg Potassium, 6g Total
Carbohydrate (6g Sugars), and 4g Protein.
**Percent Daily Values are based on a 2,000 calorie diet.
Your values may be higher or lower depending...
***Percent Daily Value for...

When shopping for food, checking food labels is crucial in controlling one's weight. It's important to know exactly what is going into your body.

lean meats, poultry, fish, beans, eggs, and nuts. The plan should also be low in saturated fats, trans fats, cholesterol, salt (sodium), and added sugars. If you are a vegetarian, vegan, or have special dietary needs, seeking professional advice will ensure that your body gets what it needs.

Making Smart "Shopping" Choices

When shopping for fresh fruits, don't get stuck in a rut by always choosing the same things. Try something exotic like a mango, kiwi, or juicy pineapple. If the fruits that one enjoys cannot be found in the fresh produce section, try the frozen food section. They can also be purchased in a can or dried, although these forms are not as healthful as fresh fruits. Check the labels to make sure that the sugar content is not too high. It is better to choose canned fruits that are packed in their own juices or water, not in syrup.

If it seems like vegetables are boring, try something new. Grilling the vegetables or steaming them and adding herbs like basil or rosemary can give zip to plain vegetables. If you are in a hurry and don't have time to prepare fresh vegetables, try canned or frozen ones. Choose ones without added salt, butter, or cream sauces. Make it a challenge to try a new vegetable every other week.

Choosing foods that are rich in calcium is important for building strong bones. Some calcium-rich foods include milk, cheese, and yogurt. When buying these items, be sure to check the labels and fat content. If a cheese is high in fat, plan on eating less of it or see if there is a lower-fat version. When trying to control your weight, go with 1 or 2 percent milk instead of drinking whole milk. Sometimes making a small change in your diet can make a huge difference. For people who are lactose-intolerant, good dairy substitutions include almond, coconut, and rice milk. Soy products are also very popular and widely available. Just be sure to again double-check the sugar content. Here are some tips when going grocery shopping that will aid in controlling your weight:

- Shop when you're not hungry. This strategy will help you resist the temptation to buy a lot of sugary sweets or other junk food.
- Plan ahead and make a list before you get to the grocery store. There are so many tasty and healthy recipes that can be found online. If you don't have access to a computer at home or at school, check your local library to see if you can use one there.
- Read the labels on all food you buy. If it is high in sugar and sodium, it probably isn't good for you and will not help you maintain your weight.

Trying to maintain a healthy weight does not mean that sweets and treats need to be eliminated completely from your diet. It may just mean eating them less often and eating smaller portions. That is why talking to a health care professional and coming up with goals and a meal plan will help.

Ten Great Questions
to Ask a Doctor

1 What is the right weight for my height?

2 Aside from appearance, why is it good to lose weight?

3 How do I set realistic and healthy weight-loss goals for myself?

4 What kinds of practical exercises can I do to help control my weight?

5 What are some common roadblocks, or things that would get in the way, of losing or maintaining my weight?

6 Who is a good person to ask to be a mentor in helping me maintain my weight?

7 What can I use to help me mark my progress?

8 What are the best foods for me to eat while trying to lose or maintain my weight?

9 Should I meet with a dietician if I need to lose a significant amount of weight?

10 How often should I weigh myself?

Chapter 3

How Exercise Can Help

Exercising, even if it is just a thirty-minute walk around the neighborhood, will help get a person out of the house and on his or her way to a healthy lifestyle. Some great forms of exercise that young adults can do by themselves or with others are biking, jogging, or playing tennis, basketball, or volleyball. If a person keeps his or her body moving, he or she is using the energy from the foods that he or she eats. That is why it is important to eat healthy foods—so that one has a good amount of energy to keep going.

Exercising also helps the body control weight. When the body is in any sort of motion, it uses up the energy that is stored as fat. When a person consumes the same amount of calories that he or she burns off, it is easy to maintain the same weight. If there are too many calories and the excess is not burned off, a person tends to gain weight. Therefore, if someone eats foods high in fat occasionally, or as a special reward, it is important to continue with a regular exercise program or maybe step it up a notch the next day. When someone wants to watch his or her weight, it is important to maintain a proper balance between calories put in and calories burned off.

Any form of exercise that gets the heart pumping can help control weight. The main thing is that a person has fun while exercising, as

Find ways to exercise, or sports that interest and motivate you, to keep the body moving and the heart pumping.

opposed to feeling obligated to do it. There are many options when it comes to forms of exercise. The possibilities are endless. The key is finding something that you take pleasure in doing. Another great way to get motivated to exercise is to take a friend along or join a team where there are new people who you can meet. With that comes the possibility of making new friends and the opportunity to learn something new.

Anything in excess is not good, whether it be food or an exercise regimen. Make sure that when starting a new exercise program or joining a team, you have the right equipment. It would also be beneficial to talk with someone or do a little research before attempting something new so that one is educated about the demands of the sport or exercise program. As always, check with an adult or seek advice from a health care professional if there is a sense of uncertainty.

Strength and Cardio Training

According to Susan Campbell, a strength and conditioning specialist, controlling or losing weight is most effectively accomplished by using strength training in conjunction with high-intensity cardio intervals.

Strength training is body-weight exercises done with or without added resistance in a circuit-style fashion. Some examples of body-weight exercises include various forms of squats, push-ups, chin-ups, planks, jumps, rows, mountain climbing, and squat thrusts.

When a person combines the above exercises in a circuit-style format, the body will really burn calories and shed fat and unused energy in the body.

Circuit training is a fun way to add variety to an exercise regime. It is also fun to do with other people.

Here is an example of a circuit-training workout using body-weight exercises:

- Jumping jacks for thirty seconds
- Body-weight squats for fifteen seconds
- Push-ups for fifteen seconds
- Squat thrusts for fifteen seconds
- Reverse lunge, eight with each leg
- Plank position for thirty seconds
- Return to jumping jacks for thirty seconds
- One dead-leg lift, eight with each leg
- Mountain climbers, ten with each leg
- Squat thrusts for fifteen seconds

Complete this list of exercises with little or no rest in between each one. Rest for two minutes, and then repeat the circuit two more times. It is called circuit training because you are repeating the same exercises.

High-intensity cardio intervals are short bursts of high-intensity activity. High-intensity cardio intervals should be completed after the body-weight exercise circuit. Here is an example of what the intervals could look like:

- Jumping jacks for twenty seconds, with a ten-second rest
- Fast mountain climbers for twenty seconds, with a ten-second rest
- Run in place for twenty seconds, with a ten-second rest
- Squat thrusts for twenty seconds, with a ten-second rest
- Back to jumping jacks for twenty seconds, with a ten-second rest

- Fast mountain climbers for twenty seconds, with a ten-second rest
- Run in place for twenty seconds, with a ten-second rest
- Squat thrusts for twenty seconds, with a ten-second rest

Always remember to do a thorough warm-up prior to exercise, as well as cool down when the workout is completed. Both of these should include some light activity, such as a short walk or a light jog and stretching. This type of workout should not be completed more than three times per week. The great thing about this suggested workout is that it is free: It requires no equipment or a gym membership. These exercises can be easily performed inside or outside. On off days, fun physical activities should be done, such as basketball, swimming, or bike riding.

Exercise helps control weight because calories are burned every time the body moves. Practically every food and drink that we consume contains calories. Calories are really a form of energy and are used to fuel everything that our bodies do, from walking to brushing our teeth to sleeping. If we consume more calories than our bodies need, the unused energy will get stored as fat for use at a later time. Therefore, to control weight, we must use any extra energy by doing physical activity.

Mind and Body Exercises

Mind and body exercises help increase muscle strength and flexibility, along with helping to alleviate stress. Young adults live in a fast-paced world filled with school pressures, competitive sports and other activities, lessons, technology, and parents with busy schedules. Just having one of these things going on in a person's life is enough to

Mind and body exercises, such as yoga, give the body strength and flexibility but also help to rest the mind, which is important in today's fast-paced society.

cause stress. The effects of stress can cause a person to not take care of himself or herself. Some people may eat more or less and might not feel as motivated to be active when they are feeling stress. These factors can make it difficult when trying to maintain a certain weight. Some great types of mind-body exercises are yoga, Pilates, and tai chi. These can all help alleviate the negative effects of stress.

Doing mind-body exercises such as yoga, Pilates, and tai chi allow a person to connect more deeply with his or her inner self and develop more confidence. The mind as well as the body should be given time to rest. When mind-body exercises are practiced, young adults develop better concentration, and their sense of calm increases.

When young adults have greater flexibility, strength, and coordination, they are more confident when trying new exercises and physical activities such as sports. The body is ready to go into full motion, and it has the ability to move freely. One is also more aware of his or her body and what it is capable of achieving. When the body isn't active, it can stiffen and it becomes more difficult to get it in motion.

Daily Activities That Help Control Weight

Believe it or not, doing daily activities like raking leaves, sweeping the floor, or cleaning the house can help you control your weight. These types of activities get the body moving. When the body is moving, calories are burned off. It is also a great way to earn money. Ask a neighbor or friend if he or she needs his or her house cleaned, yard raked, or lawn mowed. Dog walking is another excellent way to burn calories and get something accomplished at the same time. When activities like these are included in a daily routine, you will be surprised at the amount of exercise you get.

Keep on Moving

A fun way to find out how many calories one has burned is to get a pedometer and wear it throughout the day. It is amazing the amount of steps that a person takes in one day. Make it a fun challenge by trying to beat the amount of steps taken each day or each week. The American Heart Association recommends gradually adding just 250 steps per day averaged out over the week. That will give you a good start on a healthy routine of physical activity. Most sedentary adults take only 2,500 to 3,500 steps a day. Try to add between four thousand and six thousand steps to whatever you are doing now, for a total of ten thousand or more steps each day. The more steps you take, the better. Whether it is a structured exercise program, organized sport, mind-body exercises, or everyday chores, there are so many ways to control weight through movement. Finding people to do these things with makes it even more fun. Make sure you are motivated and enjoying what you are doing so that you don't get bored and/or feel obligated to "exercise."

Positive Body Image

As a young adult, your body is growing and changing constantly. Having strong bones and muscles will help the body grow at a healthy rate and build a strong foundation as it grows. Having a healthy body image is important during this time period, too. It is a topic that boys and girls start to become aware of at a young age. Body image is the way one thinks about his or her physical appearance. According to *Body Drama*, by Dr. Angelina Diaz, "A person with a 'great' body image feels comfortable and confident with her body most of the

Having a healthy body image means being able to look in the mirror and feel positive about one's reflection.

time, while a person with a 'bad' body image thinks of herself as ugly or unattractive and feels insecure about her body most of the time." When a person has a positive body image, he or she is able to discern what one should look like versus what society and media tells people to look like.

The media tell us that we all need to have perfect bodies. However, to be realistic, no one person is perfect. Everybody has days where he or she does not feel good about his or her body. A healthy way to deal with those days is to change your thinking when you're feeling bad and do things that make you feel good about who you are. Some suggestions are to go for a bike ride, call a friend, or make a list of all the things that are positive in life.

MYTHS and FACTS

MYTH

FACT

To lose weight, you need to eat three times a day and not allow yourself to snack.

When eating you want to keep track of you caloric intake. If you are taking in more calories than you are burning off, you will gain weight. As long as you're keeping track of your caloric intake, it's good to eat several smaller meals throughout the day to maintain your metabolism.

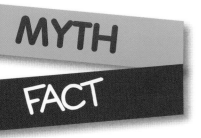

MYTH

FACT

Carbohydrates make you fat.

Carbohydrates are part of a balanced diet. It is the kind of carbohydrates that you consume that you need to be careful of. It is the fat and sugar content in the carbohydrates that can make a person gain weight.

MYTH

FACT

Avoid eating foods with fat in them.

Fats keep you fuller longer and it is not something one should avoid. Eliminating the fat will increase your hunger and also take flavor from your food. The key is to balance foods that have more fat with those that have less fat.

Chapter 4

Other Healthy Habits to Control Weight

Another thing to think about when trying to control weight is to make sure one is drinking lots of water. When water is consumed instead of soda or other sugar-sweetened drinks, it helps a person reduce the amount of calories that the body is taking in.

For instance, the average amount of calories in a regular 12-ounce can of soda is about 150, as opposed to any amount of regular water, which contains zero calories. Young people who consume one or more 12-ounce (355 milliliter) sweetened soft drinks per day are 60 percent more likely to be obese.

Not only do caffeinated beverages contain empty calories (calories that don't provide adequate nutrients), but kids who fill up on them also don't get the vitamins and minerals that they need from healthy sources. And though drinking juice may sound like it's a healthy alternative to soft drinks, juices are also loaded with sugar. Make sure you check the sugar content and number of calories. Opt for low-sugar juices, or fill your glass with half juice and half water. When these drinks are cut out, the average young adult does not make up for them by eating or drinking more calories elsewhere. Such a strategy helps in controlling weight by eliminating unnecessary calories to a person's diet.

Snacking on healthy foods is essential to controlling weight and hunger so there is less of a tendency to "pig out" during meals.

Take Responsibility for Controlling Your Own Weight

One should take responsibility for controlling his or her weight. The teen years are a time when healthy habits are formed and can be carried into adulthood. Taking ownership of the choices made when it comes to eating and exercise can give people the confidence of knowing that they can do this on their own and not have someone do it for them. This is important for young adults as they start to claim a sense of identity. As the saying goes: "Knowledge is power."

Snacking to Stay Fit

Snacking is another way to take control of your weight. Most young adults have early lunches and then attend after-school activities or have a long bus ride home. By the time they walk through the door, their stomachs are rumbling, but dinner may not be for another couple of hours. That is why snack vending machines do so well in schools. Growing bodies need constant nutrition. That is why it is important to make sure that what you are snacking on is healthy. Making a list of healthy snacks to keep in the house is a great plan. If there is no time to prepare snacks during the week, take some time over the weekend to make some fun and healthy treats. Place them in Tupperware containers or plastic storage bags for a ready-to-eat after-school snack. Choose items that are low in fat, salt, and sugar. Some good examples are fresh fruit, whole-grain crackers, plain popcorn, and mixed nuts that are unsalted. Snacking can be a good thing when healthy food is in the mix. Otherwise, you are adding unnecessary calories that will increase your weight.

When you have the knowledge about how to control your weight, you have the power to stay healthy for the rest of your life. Also, sharing the knowledge that you've gained with the surrounding community can ensure healthy living. When you read about a topic that a person may be struggling with or want to know more about, the act of reading can motivate you and give you new ideas or strategies. Education is the key to success.

Giving the Body Rest

The body needs time to recharge, just like your iPod or cell phone. After running around all day, sleep is what recharges our bodies. The body needs to plug into a bed and rest so that it has time to repair itself. Just as a person becomes frustrated when his or her iPod is only half-charged for a long trip, the body needs to be fully charged in order to function the way it should. Otherwise, it can wear down midway through the day. Although it may be fun to have sleepovers and stay up as late as you can once in a while, you should get enough sleep during the rest of the week. According to the Centers for Disease Control and Prevention, young adults need more sleep than adults. Often, young adults receive less sleep due to a full schedule that may include after-school activities, a heavy homework load, and late-night Internet use or television watching. The National Sleep Foundation recommends that children ages five to twelve years old get nine to eleven hours of sleep per night, while adolescents ages eleven to seventeen get eight-and-a-half to nine-and-a-half hours each night.

When a person is well rested, he or she has more energy throughout the day to perform activities and do exercise. The body has the

According to KidsHealth.org, young adults need about eight to nine-and-a-half hours of sleep a night to function properly and give the body the time it needs to restore, rebuild, and grow.

energy to work off the calories consumed. When you don't get enough sleep, your body will feel sluggish, and you won't have as much enthusiasm to go out and exercise.

Positive Peers

Finding positive peers will also help a person to control his or her weight. Young adults listen to each other and watch what their peers are doing. They are increasingly aware of what friends and people around them are thinking and doing. Young adults tend not to listen as much to their parents or to health care professionals. Growing adolescents need support and encouragement from friends and family members. It is kind of like going to a big race: When friends and family cheer in support, there is more motivation to finish and do it well. The same goes with building healthy habits to control weight. A person is more likely to continue with healthy habits if there are so many supportive people. A fun way to build healthy habits with peers is to find and make recipes together. When people find friends who make healthy choices, they also tend to make healthy choices. Finding friends who are different from you can give you a new perspective on methods to control your weight. Friends can open the mind to new things because not everyone likes to do the same things.

Balancing Schoolwork and Life

Schoolwork can pile up, and social life can get quite busy between school activities and friends. This can affect a person's weight by making it harder to fit physical activity into a person's schedule. It is important to balance schoolwork, social life, and physical activity

If schoolwork is weighing you down, find ways to break it up. Try doing twenty to thirty minutes of schoolwork and then twenty or thirty minutes of exercise or something creative.

with downtime for oneself. When people get too stressed out, some tend to overeat to compensate for it or not eat because there are just so many things to do. They either forget or are too nervous to even think about eating. Make sure to take breaks from schoolwork and do something enjoyable, even if it is just for a few minutes. Call a friend, do a crossword puzzle, go for a walk, read a magazine, ride a bike, write a letter to an older relative, or try and find a new and healthy recipe online to cook for the next meal. In life, there will always be things to do. The key is to find balance. Exercise is a great way to release tension that can build up. Avoiding people who make you feel stressed or angry is also a good way to lessen stress. If you are struggling with how to deal with stress, talk to an adult or a professional who can help.

Taking Time Out for Yourself

Taking time out of this busy, fast-paced world is a good way to stay healthy as well. Find time to meditate, write in a journal, or read a good book. Living in such a technologically advanced world makes it hard to disconnect. Unplugging the brain from the Internet, video games, and television is good for the mind and gives it a chance to rest and reflect on what is important in life. Meditation allows any stress or tension to clear away for a time. A person does not have to sit and meditate for hours in order to see results. It could just be sitting quietly for a few minutes and thinking about something that makes him or her happy. Writing one's thoughts down in a journal is also an excellent way to sort out feelings or situations that may be going on in life. Drawing can also be a great way to escape if a person does not like to write. Anything that

Taking time out to just sit and daydream or meditate is good for the body and soul because it gives the body a break from all the chaos going on in the world.

allows the mind to rest and escape the business of daily life can help the body rest. Giving the body time to rest recharges the brain and muscles and gives them time to repair before starting all over again the next day.

Many Ways to Control Your Weight

There is a wealth of information in books and online about how to maintain a healthy weight. The key is to find sources that are reliable and thoroughly researched. It is also important to seek a health care professional's advice if you feel like you need to lose or gain weight. Controlling one's weight is something that a person has to think about for his or her entire life. There will always be societal pressures to make a person feel that he or she needs to look or feel a certain way. Make sure that as a young adult, you feel positive about who you are and what you want in life, and surround yourself with those who support you.

GLOSSARY

body image The way one thinks about his or her physical appearance.

caloric intake The total number of calories that a person consumes.

calorie The unit of measure for the energy value of food.

complex carbohydrates Starchy foods that are good sources of energy and nutrients, such as bread, rice, pasta, and grains.

exercise regimen A regulated system of exercise.

health care professional A physician, nurse, nutritionist, therapist, or other individual trained in an area of health care delivery and directly involved in providing clinical care to patients.

hormone A chemical substance made in one part of the body that travels through the bloodstream and affects cells and tissues in another part of the body.

meditate To contemplate; to sit or lie down and come to a deep rest while still remaining conscious.

mind and body exercises Exercises that are designed to give the mind a rest as movements are made with the body.

nutrients The proteins, carbohydrates, fats, vitamins, and minerals that are provided by food and are necessary for growth and the maintenance of life.

nutritional value The amount of actual nutrition that is contained within a food or liquid substance.

nutritionist A health care professional with special training in nutrition. He or she can offer help with the choice of foods that a person eats and drinks; also called a dietitian.

physician A physician, medical practitioner, doctor of medicine, or medical doctor who practices medicine and is concerned with maintaining or restoring human health.

Pilates A series of gentle, muscle-strengthening exercises formulated by Dr. Joseph Pilates.

protein An essential nutrient that helps build many parts of the body, including muscle, bone, skin, and blood.

registered dietician A health care professional with an extensive scientific background in food, nutrition, biochemistry, and physiology.

role model Someone worthy of imitation.

saturated fats The fats that are found in meat and other animal products, such as butter, cheese, and milk (except skim milk).

sedentary lifestyle A type of lifestyle that is lacking adequate physical exercise.

simple carbohydrates Refined sugars, such as white sugar.

social discrimination Discriminatory or abusive behavior toward peers.

tai chi A Chinese system of slow meditative exercise designed for relaxation, balance, and health.

trans fats The unhealthy fats that are found in margarine and snack foods, baked goods, and fried foods; also called hydrogenated or partially hydrogenated fats.

unsaturated fats The healthier fats that are found in plant foods, certain oils, and fish.

yoga A healing system involving a combination of breathing exercises, physical postures, and meditation.

Action for Healthy Kids
4711 West Golf Road, Suite 625
Skokie, IL 60076
(800) 416-5136
Web site: http://www.actionforhealthykids.org
This national nonprofit organization is dedicated to addressing the
epidemic of overweight, undernourished, and sedentary youth by
focusing on changes in schools.

Active Healthy Kids Canada
2 Bloor Street East, Suite #1804
Toronto, ON M4W 1A8
Canada
(416) 913-0238
Web site: http://www.activehealthykids.ca
Active Healthy Kids Canada strives to be a trusted source for
knowledge that influences the thinking and action of issue stake-
holders in order to help them build better programs, campaigns,
and policies that will increase physical activity among youth.

American Dietetic Association
120 South Riverside Plaza, Suite 2000
Chicago, IL 60606-6995
(800) 877-1600
Web site: http://www.eatright.org
This is the nation's largest organization of food and nutrition professionals. It serves the public by promoting optimal nutrition,
health, and well being.

Canadian Partnership for Children's Health & Environment
130 Spadina Avenue, Suite 301
Toronto, ON M5V 2L4
Canada
(819) 458-3750
Web site: http://www.healthyenvironmentforkids.ca
This is a multisectoral collaboration of twelve organizations with
    expertise in issues related to children, health, public health and
    the environment.

Healthy Kids, Healthy Communities
University of North Carolina at Chapel Hill
400 Market Street Suite 205
Chapel Hill, NC 27516
(919) 843-2523
Web site: http://www.healthykidshealthycommunities.org
The primary goal of this national program of the Robert Wood
    Johnson Foundation is to implement healthy eating and active
    living policy and environmental change initiatives that can support
    healthier communities for American children and families.

Kids Health from Nemours
10140 Centurion Parkway
Jacksonville, FL 32256
(904) 697-4100
Web site: http://kidshealth.org
KidsHealth is a part of the Nemours Foundation's Center for
    Children's Health Media. It provides information on health and

offers perspective, advice, and comfort about a wide range of physical, emotional, and behavioral issues that affect children and teens.

Vegetarian Resource Group
P.O. Box 1463, Dept. IN
Baltimore, MD 21203
(410) 366-VEGE (8343)
Web site: http://www.vrg.org
This nonprofit organization is dedicated to educating the public about vegetarianism and the interrelated issues of health, nutrition, ecology, ethics, and world hunger.

Web Sites

Due to the changing nature of Internet links, Rosen Publishing has developed an online list of Web sites related to the subject of this book. This site is updated regularly. Please use this link to access the list:

http://www.rosenlinks.com/hab/weight

Bartell, Susan S. *Dr. Susan's Girls-Only Weight Loss Guide: The Easy, Fun Way to Look and Feel Good*. Williston Park, NY: Parent Positive Press, 2006.

Beck, Leslie. *Healthy Eating for Preteens and Teens*. Toronto, Canada: Penguin, 2005.

Christopher, Matt. *Run for It*. New York, NY: Little, Brown & Company, 2008.

CosmoGIRL. *Ask Cosmo Girl About Nutrition and Fitness*. New York, NY: Hearst Books, 2008.

Davis, Debi. *Back Off! I'll Lose Weight When I'm Ready*. Hollywood: FL: Frederick Fell Publishing, 2004.

Ellin, Abby. *Teenage Waistland: A Former Fat Kid Weighs in on Living Large, Losing Weight, and How Parents Can (and Can't) Help*. New York, NY: Perseus Publishing, 2007.

Fletcher, Anne M. *Weight Loss Confidential: How Teens Lose Weight and Keep It Off—and What They Wish Parents Knew*. Boston, MA: Houghton Mifflin Company, 2006.

Gould, Pamela, and Eleanor P. Taylor. *Feeding the Kids: The Flexible, No-Battles, Healthy Eating System for the Whole Family*. Colorado Springs, CO: Mancala Publishing, 2007.

Kirberger, Kimberley. *No Body's Perfect: Stories by Teens About Body Image, Self-Acceptance, and the Search for Identity*. New York, NY: Scholastic, 2003.

McCoy, Kathy, and Charles Wibblesmann. *Growing and Changing: A Handbook for Pre-Teens*. New York, NY: Perigee Books, 2003.

Rockwell, Lizzy. *Good Enough to Eat: A Kid's Guide to Food and Nutrition*. New York, NY: HarperCollins, 2009.

BIBLIOGRAPHY

American Heart Association. "How Do You Maintain Weight Loss?" Retrieved June 20, 2009 (http://www.americanheart.org/presenter.jhtml?identifier=3040451).

Beck, Leslie. *Healthy Eating for Preteens and Teens*. Toronto, Canada: Penguin, 2005.

Carmichael, Chris. *Chris Carmichael's Food for Fitness: Eat Right to Train Right*. New York, NY: Berkley Books, 2004.

Centers for Disease Control and Prevention. "Are You Getting Enough Sleep?" Retrieved June 20, 2009 (http://www.cdc.gov/Partners/Archive/Sleep).

Centers for Disease Control and Prevention. "Tips for Parents—Ideas to Help Children Maintain a Healthy Weight." Retrieved June 20, 2009 (http://www.cdc.gov/healthyweight/children).

Diaz, Angelina. *Body Drama*. New York, NY: Gotham Books 2008.

Fletcher, Anne M. *Weight Loss Confidential: How Teens Lose Weight and Keep It Off—and What They Wish Parents Knew*. Boston, MA: Houghton Mifflin Company, 2006.

Gavin, Mary. "Learning About Carbohydrates." February 2008. Retrieved September 20,2009 (http://kidshealth.org/kid/nutrition/food/carb.html#).

Gavin, Mary. "Learning About Proteins." February 2008. Retrieved September 20, 2009 (http://kidshealth.org/kid/nutrition/food/protein.html#).

Gavin, Mary. "What's the Right Weight for Me?" September 2008. Retrieved July 16, 2009. (http://kidshealth.org/kid/talk/qa/fat_thin.html#).

Haduch, Bill. *Food Rules*. New York, NY: Dutton Children's Books, 2001.

Hall, Ross Hume. *The Unofficial Guide to Smart Nutrition*. New York, NY: IDG Books Worldwide, Inc., 2000.

Kuklierus, Ann, and Gloria Mayer. *What to Do for Teen Health*. La Habra, CA: IHA, 2008.

National Center for Chronic Prevention and Health Promotion. *Chronic Disease Notes & Reports*, Vol. 12, No. 2, Spring/ Summer 1999.

Nemours Foundation. "Caffeine and Your Child." Retrieved September 20, 2009 (http://www.uofmchildrenshospital.org/ kidshealth/article.aspx?artid=40419).

Neumark-Sztainer, Dianne. *"I'm, Like, So Fat": Helping Your Teen Make Healthy Choices About Eating and Exercise in a Weight-Obsessed World*. New York, NY: Guilford Press, 2005.

Wenig, Marsha. "Yoga for Kids." Retrieved September 25, 2009. (http://www.yogajournal.com/lifestyle/210).

WIN (Weight-Control Information Network). "Physical Activity and Weight Control." November 2006. Retrieved July 8, 2009 (http:// win.niddk.nih.gov/publications/physical.htm).

INDEX

About the Author

Kate Canino is an author and educator living in Rochester, New York. A graduate of the College of Saint Rose in childhood education, Canino always promotes a healthy lifestyle by being a positive role model for kids. She maintains her weight through walking, biking, and playing racquetball and tennis, and she hopes to take up rock climbing in the spring. She enjoys cooking and finding healthy new and creative recipes to share with her friends and family. She is also working on writing grants for ARTWalk about teaching kids how to cook and eat healthy.

Photo Credits

Cover Shutterstock.com; p. 5 Melanie Stetson Freeman/Christian Science Monitor/Getty Images; p. 8 Jose Luis Pelaez, Inc./Blend Images/Getty Images; p. 10 © www.istockphoto.com/Nancy Louie; pp. 12, 17, 20, 22–23, 24–25, 35, 38, 41 Shutterstock.com; p. 15 Karan Kapoor/Stone/Getty Images; p. 26 © www.istockphoto.com/Radu Razvan; p. 28 © www.istockphoto.com/RiverNorthPhotography; p. 33 © www.istockphoto.com/Jennifer Trenchard; p. 45 © www.istockphoto.com/Kelly Cline; p. 48 © www.istockphoto.com/Bob Ingelhart; p. 50 © www.istockphoto.com/Elena Elisseeva; p. 52 © www.istockphoto.com/Amanda Rohde.

Designer: Nicole Russo; Editor: Nicholas Croce;
Photo Researcher: Amy Feinberg